DATE DUE

MAY 3 0 2013			
JAN 2 7 2017			
OCT 1 1 2023			

FOLLETT

Spot the Shape

Shapes in Music

Rebecca Rissman

Heinemann Library
Chicago, Illinois

© 2009 Heinemann Library
an imprint of Capstone Global Library, LLC
Chicago, Illinois

Customer Service: 888-454-2279

Visit our website at www.heinemannraintree.com

Designed by Joanna Hinton-Malivoire
Photo research by Tracy Cummins and Heather Mauldin
Color Reproduction by Dot Gradtions Ltd, UK
Printed and bound by South China Printing Company Ltd

13 12 11 10 09
10 9 8 7 6 5 4 3 2 1

Library of Congress Cataloging-in-Publication Data
Rissman, Rebecca.
Shapes in music / Rebecca Rissman.
p. cm. -- (Spot the shape!)
Includes bibliographical references and index.
ISBN 978-1-4329-2171-2 (hc) -- ISBN 978-1-4329-2177-4 (pb) 1. Shapes--Juvenile literature. I. Title.
QA445.5.R5725 2008
516'.15--dc22
                              2008043209

Acknowledgments
The author and publishers are grateful to the following for permission to reproduce copyright material: ©AGE Fotostock pp. **6** (P. Narayan), **13** (Hemera), **14** (Hemera); ©Alamy pp. **4** (George and Monserrate Schwartz), **7** (Image Source Ltd), **8** (Image Source Ltd), **11** (D. Hurst), **12** (D. Hurst), **21** (Mode Images Limited); ©Getty Images pp. **15** (Steve Shott), **16** (Steve Shott), **23c** (Steve Shott); ©Jupiter Images pp. **9** (Ablestock.com), **10** (Ablestock.com), **23b** (Ablestock.com); ©Peter Arnold Inc pp. **17** (JorgenSchytte), **18** (JorgenSchytte); ©Shutterstock pp. **19** (Jakez), **20** (Jakez), **23a** (Jakez).

Cover photograph of colourful Mexican guitars in a souvenir shop reproduced with permission of ©Getty Images/Jan Tyler. Back cover photograph of a balalaika reproduced with permission of ©Jupiter Images (Ablestock.com).

Contents

Shapes

Shapes are all around us.

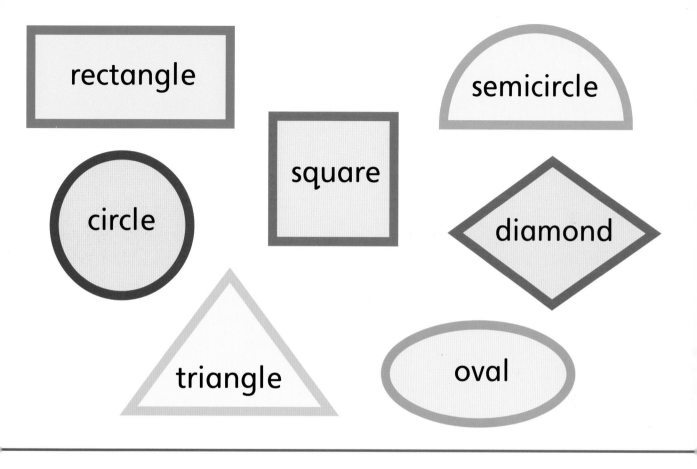

Each shape has a name.

Shapes in Music

There are many shapes in music.

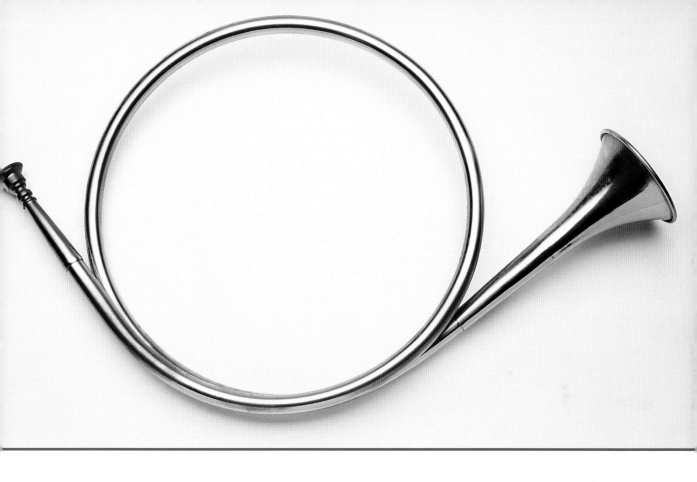

What shape can you see in this horn?

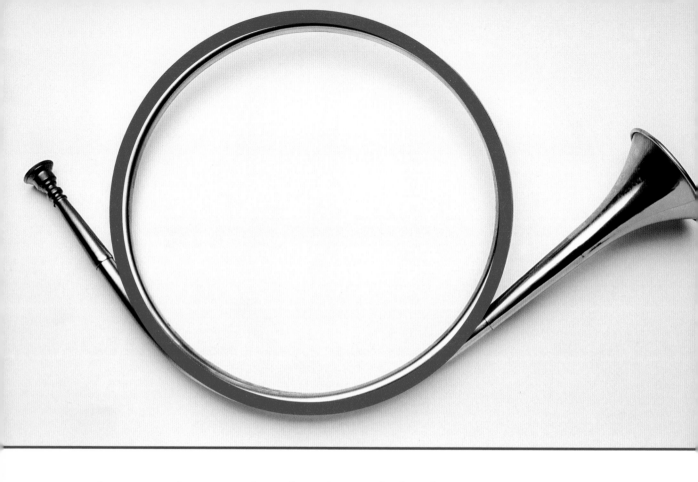

There is a circle in this horn.

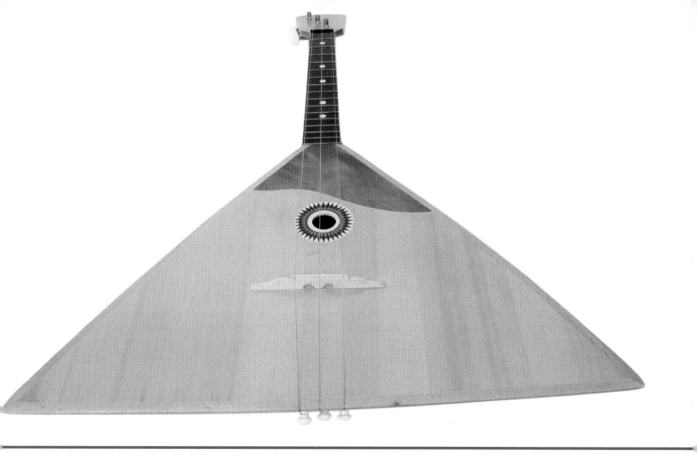

What shape can you see in this balalaika?

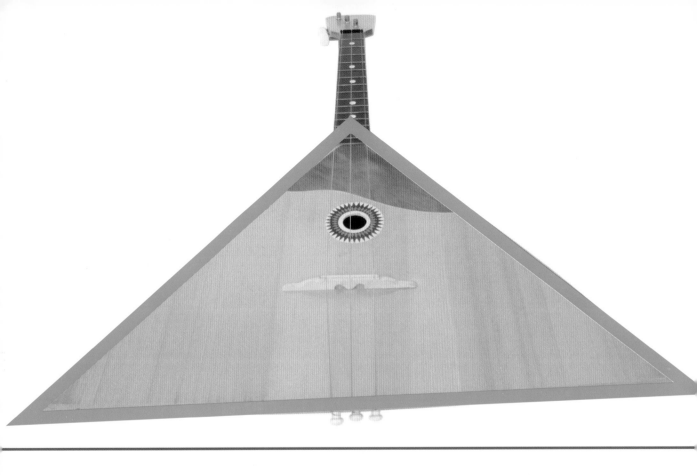

There is a triangle in this balalaika.

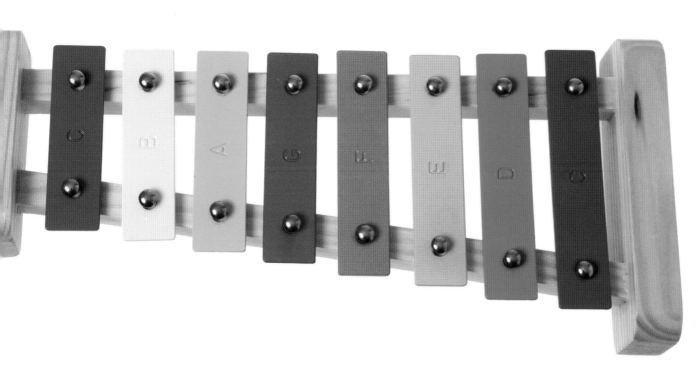

What shapes can you see on
this xylophone?

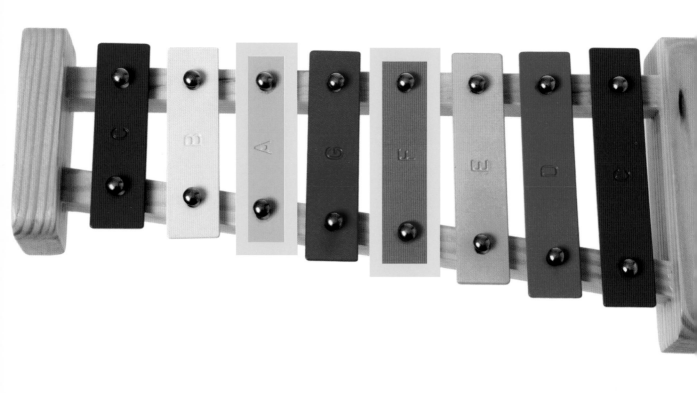

There are rectangles on this xylophone.

What shape can you see in
this tambourine?

There is a semicircle in this tambourine.

What shape can you see in
these maracas?

There are ovals in these maracas.

What shape can you see in
this masenqo?

There is a square in this masenqo.

What shape can you see on
this accordion?

There is a diamond on this accordion.

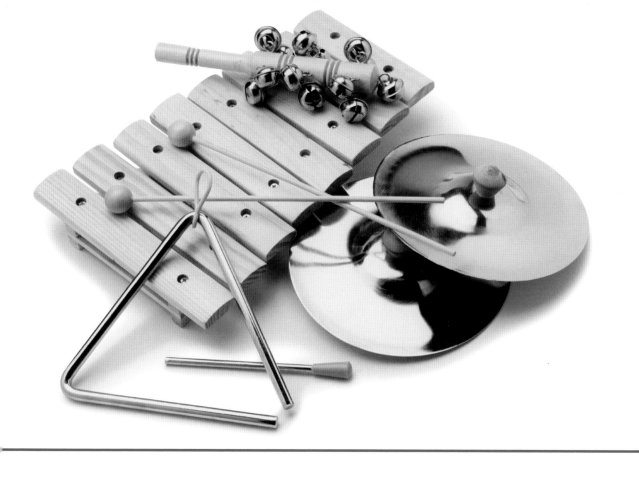

There are many shapes in music.
What shapes do you see?

Naming Shapes

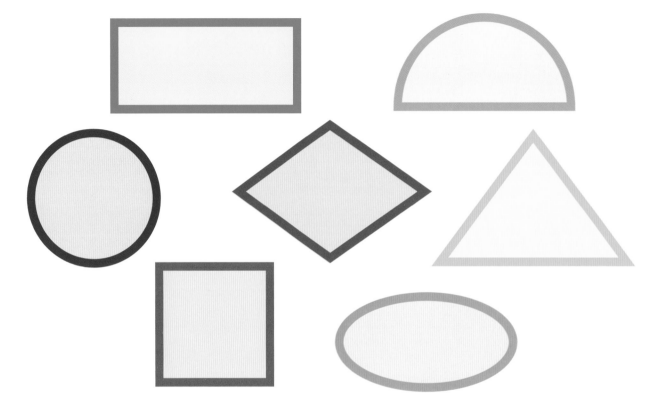

Can you remember the names of these shapes?

Picture Glossary

accordion instrument that you squeeze in and out to play

balalaika Russian instrument like a guitar

masenqo Ethiopian instrument like a violin

xylophone instrument made of wooden or metal bars that make different notes when hit

Index

Note to Parents and Teachers
Before reading
Make a simple handout showing the outlines of a square, rectangle, triangle, circle, oval, semicircle, and diamond. Ask children to write the name of the shape inside the outline. Using page 5, help children to check their answers.

After reading
• Instruments: show children the collection of musical instruments on page 6 and make a list of all the shapes that they can find in the instruments. Which shape did they find the most?
• Make shape shakers: fill an empty shoebox, oatmeal container, pasta box, and other geometrically shaped containers with dry rice or beans to create simple percussion instruments. Then, invite children to decorate their shakers with cut-out shapes or drawings of shapes.